AMERICAN SYMBOLS

The Seals and Flags of the Fifty States

By M. B. SCHNAPPER

PUBLIC AFFAIRS PRESS, WASHINGTON, D. C.

FOR AMY AND ERIC

Copyright, 1974, by M. B. Schnapper
Published by Public Affairs Press
419 New Jersey Ave., S.E., Washington, D. C. 20003
Printed in the United States of America
Library of Congress Catalog Card No. 74-76281
ISBN 8183-128

PREFACE

This book is based chiefly on information and facsimiles provided by the governors of the states, official archivists, historical societies, the Army's Institute of Heraldry, and the Library of Congress.

Among those who assisted in the preparation of the work are Edgar Morgan, former Washington representative of New Jersey, Walter B. Wheeler, Rolfe W. Larson, Allen Babuska, Strod Bock, and A. Guy Hope.

It is to the great credit of the Daughters of the American Revolution and the American Legion, particularly of their state affiliates, that interest in the history of American flags and seals has been kept alive during much of the nation's recent history

M. B. SCHNAPPER

Washington, D. C.

CONTENTS

The front and back of the U. S. Seal.

INTRODUCTION

While much has been written about American flags, the official seals of the nation and the states have received negligible attention although they tell us far more about our country than flags. It is for this reason that the present book is primarily focused on seals—their origin, purpose, and significance.

As is readily evident in the pages that follow, official seals are more than merely patriotic emblems. They embody, symbolically and factually, the ideals, traditions, and history of the United States during the past two hundred years.

It is indicative of the importance of seals that on the very day that the Declaration of Independence was proclaimed, July 4, 1776, the Continental Congress appointed a committee of great Americans—Benjamin Franklin, John Adams, and Thomas Jefferson—to "bring in a device for a seal for the United States of America."

Much to the surprise and chagrin of some delegates to the Congress, the committee recommended a design with a strong Biblical motif. It depicted a crowned Pharaoh pursuing the Israelites through the divided waters of the Red Sea; on the opposite shore stood Moses bathed in light, extending his arms toward the sea and biding the waters to swallow Pharaoh and his troops. Emblazoned around the seal was an inscription from the Old Testament: "Rebellion Against Tyranny is Obedience to God." Conceived by Franklin, the design was amended at the urging of Jefferson, who felt that the children of Israel should be shown in the wilderness under the guidance of a cloud by-day and a pillar of fire by night.

7

Since the design didn't suit the Continental Congress a new committee was set up but this group didn't come up with a satisfactory seal and so a third committee was appointed in 1782. The latter, aided by William Barton, a Philadelphian with some knowledge of heraldry, drew up several designs about which the Congress had some reservations. Finally, it was left to Charles Thomson, secretary of the legislature, to adapt ideas from these various drawings. His recommendations became the basis for the Great Seal approved by the Continental Congress on June 20, 1782, fifteen months after the Articles of Confederation became the new nation's original basis for self-government.

Virtually unchanged since 1782, the Great Seal, emblem of the nation's sovereignty, represents union of the states through the Congress, dedication to peace, capacity for national defense, and the qualities of vigilance, perseverance, and justice.

Symbolic of courage, power, and freedom, the seal's bald American eagle[1] — also known as the bald-headed eagle although its head and neck are thickly covered with white feathers—represents Congress. The sheaf of arrows stand for national defense and the olive branch desire for peace.

In the eagle's beak is a scroll inscribed with the Latin motto "E Pluribus Unum" (One Out of Many) alluding to the merger of the thirteen original colonies into an indivisible nation. This motto was adopted at the joint recommendation of Franklin, Adams, and Jefferson. There are various versions of the motto's history; the most widely accepted traces it back to the Epistles of the Roman poet Horace.

The shield's thirteen vertical stripes are derived from the flag authorized in 1777 by the Continental Congress. The horizontal segment adjoining the stripes signifies the nation.

Above the eagle is a circular crest representing the United States as a new constellation in the galaxy of nations. The thirteen stars stand for each of the founding states.

Above is a sketch based upon the Great Seal recommended to the Continental Congress by a committee composed of Benjamin Franklin, Thomas Jefferson, and John Adams. Below are designs proposed by a successor committee.

Although there are many variations of the Great Seal's design—clearly evident in symbols of Congress and the Supreme Court, in the insignia of some federal departments, in official medals and awards, in the seals of some states, and on both currency and coins—the seal proper is impressed in wax on only highly important documents signed personally by the President and countersigned by the Secretary of State (custodian of the seal) or documents signed by officials authorized by the President to affix the seal. The wax seal usually appears on Presidential proclamations, and warrants, treaties, the envelopes of communications from the President to heads of foreign governments, and the commissions of cabinet members, ambassadors, ministers, and other high officials. The design within the seal's circle also serves as the coat of arms of the United States.

The design on the seal's reverse side is symbolic of the nation's durability. The pyramid of 13 blocks represent the original states. They are shown in stone to symbolize the Union's permanence and strength. (The designer left room for several more blocks at the top but the pattern has never changed). Directly above the pyramid is the all-seeing eye of Divine Providence, a device often used during the eighteenth century. In effect the adjoining mottos express the Founding Fathers' confidence in divine blessing of the

The Great Seal's eagle evolved from these early designs.

11

United States as a democracy dedicated to the principles of freedom, justice, and liberty. The motto "Annuit Coeptis" stands for "God· Has Favored Our Undertaking"; "Novus Ordo Seclorum" means "A New Order of the Ages." Both mottos, it is believed, were suggested by lines in the Latin poetry of Virgil. The Roman numerals at the pyramid's base mark the historic year 1776.

THE AMERICAN FLAG

Although the United States is relatively speaking one of the world's younger nations, its flag is the second oldest national banner still flying. Denmark's flag, adopted in 1219, is the only one which dates back further in unchanged form.

Immediate predecessor of the Stars and Stripes was the "Grand Union Flag" under which General George Washington stood when he took command of the Continental Army at Cambridge, Massachusetts, in 1776. It had thirteen alternately red and white stripes symbolizing the colonies but the blue canton of this banner contained the crosses of St. George (England) and St. Andrew (Scotland) indicating continued ties with Great Britain. This flag was surprisingly similar to that of the British East India Company, but the red and white stripes may have been adapted from the Dutch flag which flew over New Netherlands from 1609 to 1664.

The design of the flag approved by the Continental Congress in 1777,[2] long before the Constitution was even thought of, was spelled out in a resolution stipulating that the banner should have thirteen alternately red and white stripes and thirteen white stars[3] on a blue field. George Washington described the symbolism of this flag in these words: "We take the stars from heaven, the red from our mother country, separating it by the white stripes, thus showing that we have separated from her. And the white stripes will go down to posterity representing liberty."

Legend has it that the first flag of the type authorized by

NEW ENGLAND

NEW YORK

RHODE ISLAND

CONTINENTAL FLAG

BUNKER HILL FLAG

BENNINGTON FLAG

COLONIAL FLAGS

13

the Continental Congress in 1777 was devised in the previous year by a Philadelphia seamstress, Betsy Ross. This story grew out of claims advanced by her grandson, William Canby, in a paper he read before the Pennsylvania Historical Society in 1870; his information was based on recollections of what Mrs. Ross told him when she was 84 years old and he a lad of 11.

The validity of Canby's claims were disputed by the author of this book in 1951 when the Post Office Department announced issuance of a commemorative stamp in honor of Mrs. Ross; I felt it was inappropriate for the government to celebrate what was little more than a myth. In a New York Times article of December 29, 1951, about the controversy that arose a Post Office official stated: "But even if it is a myth it is a pleasant one. It is a beautiful story that has been in all the history books and which all school children love. We can't disprove it, so why not accept it."

Fairly substantial historical facts indicate that Francis Hopkinson, a signer of the Declaration of Independence and a New Jersey delegate to the Continental Congress, probably designed the flag.

Another interesting legend is that the flag is derived from the stars and stripes in the coat of arms of Washington's family at Sulgrave Manor, England.[4]

Throughout the Revolution there were Colonial flags which used red and white stripes, stars, and the blue field in various combinations. Some included symbols such as trees, beavers, anchors, and rattlesnakes with appropriate mottos.

Trees were often associated with rebellion against Britain. An old elm in Boston's Hanover Square, where the Sons of Liberty met, was known as the Liberty Tree. A live oak in Charleston, South Carolina, was a shelter under which patriots gathered to discuss political questions and there the Declaration of Independence was read to the town's people.

The Pine Tree Flag of New England—a white flag with a

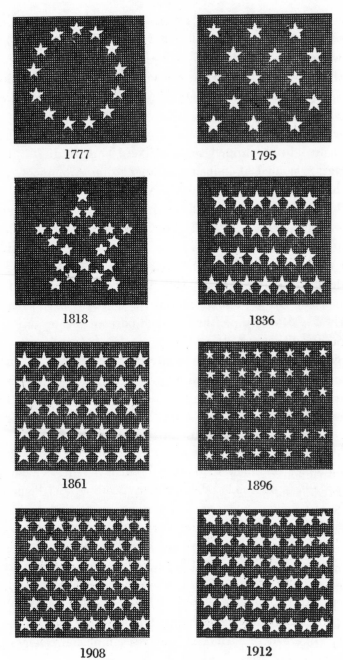

CHANGES IN THE NATIONAL FLAG.

green pine tree and the inscription "An Appeal to Heaven"—was also the ensign of Revolutionary War cruisers and a pine tree appeared in the canton of the Bunker Hill flag.

The rattlesnake theme was especially popular in the South. The slogan "Don't Tread On Me" invariably accompanied flags depicting rattlesnakes.

The beaver emblem on a plain white flag is said to have been used by the armed ships of New York in 1775. The beaver, a symbol of industry, alludes to the prominent role of the fur trade in the colony's early history. Accounts by explorer Henry Hudson of the rich harvests of furs collected by Indians of the area led Holland to authorize the establishment of trading companies in New York. The beaver symbol was used on the seal of New Netherlands and also found a place on seals of New York City and New York State. (The beaver can still be seen on the reverse side of Oregon's flag).

The flag of maritime Rhode Island bore an anchor, thirteen stars, and the word "Hope."

Strikingly similar to the Stars and Stripes was the flag carried by the Green Mountain boys at the Battle of Bennington in August, 1777. It has sometimes been asserted that the national flag was fashioned after the pattern of the Bennington flag but there is no substantiating historical data.

All of these flags disappeared soon after the national flag was adopted but some of their symbolism is still evident in the state flags of Rhode Island, South Carolina, and Pennsylvania.[5]

In 1794, several years after Vermont and Kentucky joined the Union, Congress provided for a national flag with fifteen stripes and stars,[6] but in 1818, when other states had been or were about to be admitted, it was decided that the number of stripes should be reduced permanently to thirteen to represent all states and that a star be added for each new state.[7] In all there have been twenty-seven official changes in the numbers of stars since 1777.

Today the Stars and Stripes—also known as Old Glory, the Red, White and Blue, and the Star-Spangled Banner, to mention only a few of the affectionate names by which the American flag has been known—is by law and custom the nation's most revered symbol.[8] It is never dipped to an individual, whether the President of the United States or a foreign potentate; this courtesy is observed only in mutual salutes between nations. Its care and use are carefully prescribed by the Flag Code approved by Congress in 1942.[9]

1. The eagle as a national symbol is not peculiar to the United States. Because of its prowess and magnificent majesty in flight it has since ancient times been used as an emblem of power. As far back as 5,000 years ago this huge, handsome bird was the emblem of the Mesopotamian city of Lagash (Telloh). The Byzantine rulers used a two-headed eagle to denote their control of both the East and the West.

The eagle was associated with Jupiter in Roman mythology and its figure appeared on the standards of Roman legions. It became the emblem of the Holy Roman Empire founded by Charlemagne and dissolved by Napoleon in 1806. In modern times it has been dominant in the seals and coats of arms of many nations—including Mexico, Panama, the Philippines, Russia, Germany, Poland, Spain, Albania, Austria, Ghana, Jordan, and Zambia.

When the Founding Fathers of the United States gave consideration to an appropriate national symbol some members of the Continental Congress urged the selection of the wild turkey as the national symbol and several delegates thought the dove of peace more appropriate to a nation seeking to live in harmony with all peoples.

Both naturalist John Audubon and Benjamin Franklin preferred the turkey, a truly indigenous American bird. In a letter of January 26, 1784, Franklin expressed strong objections to the honor accorded the eagle: "For my part, I wish the bald eagle had not been chosen as the representative of our country; he is a bird of bad moral character; he does not get his living honestly: you may have seen him perched on some dead tree, where, too lazy to fish for himself, he watches the labor of the fishing-hawk; and, when that diligent bird has at length taken a fish, and is bearing it to his nest for the support of his mate and young ones, the bald eagle pursues him, and takes it from him. With all this injustice he is never in good case; but, like those among men who live by sharping and robbing, he is generally poor, and often very lousy. Besides, he is a rank coward; the little kingbird, not bigger than a sparrow, attacks him boldly and drives him out of the district."

Congress, however, decided that the eagle—traditional ruler of the heights of freedom, fiercely independent and protective of its young—was an ideal symbol for the new United States of America.

Although protected by Federal law since 1940, eagles have been rapidly disappearing in recent years but they can still be seen in mountainous parts of the nation, particularly in Alaska.

2. The day on which the flag was authorized by the Continental Congress, June 14, 1777, is annually commemorated as Flag Day.

3. The star is a symbol of heaven and the stripe is symbolic of the rays of light emanating from the sun. Both themes have long been represented on the standards of nations, from the banners of the astral worshippers of ancient Egypt and Babylon to the twelve-starred flag of the Spanish Conquistadors under Cortez. In the course of time stars and stripes have also appeared on the flags of various nations of Europe, Asia, and the Americas. (See "Symbols of the Nations" by A. Guy Hope, Public Affairs Press, 1973).

4. Early American artists added to the confusion considerably by their inaccurate conceptions of the flag.

Although the Stars and Stripes had no existence when General Washington crossed the Delaware on December 25, 1776, the famous painting of that historic event by Emanuel Leutze conspicuously displays this flag.

When the Battle of Lake Erie took place in 1813, the flag had fifteen stripes, but the painting of this historic event by Nix Powell represents the flag with thirteen stripes.

5. The most authoritative and up-to-date book about old and new state flags is "The Flag Book of the United States" by Whitney Smith, William Morrow and Company, 1970.

6. It was an extraordinarily large version of this flag, 42 by 30 feet in size, which inspired a young Washington lawyer and poet, Francis Scott Key, to write "The Star Spangled Banner," which became the national anthem in 1931. During the war with England in 1814 Key went aboard a British warship to arrange for the release of an American prisoner. He was compelled to stay on the ship during the night-long bombardment of Fort McHenry near Baltimore. When firing ceased at daybreak and Key saw the

U. S. flag still waving at the fort he scribbled hastily the poem which became the basis for his famed song. An ironic but little known fact is that its music is based upon a patriotic English melody entitled "To Anacreon in Heaven."

7. Contrary to popular belief, none of the stars represents a particular state, the order of a state's adherence to the Constitution, or admission into the Union. The fifty stars represent the states collectively, not individually.

Erroneous notions arose out of the belief that an executive order issued by President William Howard Taft on June 24, 1912, recognized a public wish to give each state a definite star in the flag. His order dealt with the position of the stars and the proportions, size, and color of flags used by the federal government. No Presidential order refers to the representation of the stars on the flag. There is no more reason to suppose that the stars represent the states individually than there is to suppose that certain stripes represent particular states.

8. The Pledge of Allegiance to the flag has undergone several important changes since it was written in 1892 by Francis Bellamy, a cousin of Edward Bellamy, famed author of "Looking Backward, 2000-1887." It was composed in response to a proposal by President Benjamin Harrison that school children be encouraged to respect the flag: "The system of universal education is in our age the most important and salutary feature of the spirit of enlightenment. . . Let the National Flag float over every schoolhouse in the country, and the exercises be such as shall impress upon our youth the patriotic duties of American citizenship.' "

Francis Bellamy, a member of The Youth's Companion editorial staff, wrote the following pledge: "I pledge allegiance to my flag, and to the Republic for which it stands, one nation indivisible, with liberty and justice for all."

During the upsurge of radicalism in the 1920's some citizens objected to "my flag" on the ground that it was ambiguous to foreign-born school children. Accordingly "the Flag of the United States" was substituted for "my flag." And in 1954 President Eisenhower signed a Congressional resolution incorporating "under God" in the pledge. The present phrasing is as follows: "I pledge allegiance to the Flag of the United States of America and to the Republic for which it stands, one Nation under God, indivisible, with liberty and justice for all."

9. The text of the Flag Code appears at the end of the book.

ALABAMA

Unique among American emblems, Alabama's seal is a map of the state showing its rivers and boundaries. It was used during the first fifty years of the state's history but not formally adopted until 1939.

Between 1868 and 1939 the seal consisted of an eagle superimposed on a shield of the U. S. In the eagle's beak was a scroll with the motto "Here We Rest," supposedly the English translation of the Indian word "Alibamo" from which the state's name is derived. This seal came into use when a "carpetbag" legislature assumed control over Alabama's government.

On the shield of the state's coat of arms (above) are emblems of the five governments that have held sovereignty over Alabama at various stages of its history—Spain, France, Great Britain, the Confederacy and the United States. Facing the shield are eagles symbolic of courage. The crest is a ship of the type in which Iberville and Bienville arrived from France to settle Alabama's first colony in 1699. The ship is also a reminder of the fact that Alabama has been a maritime state. The English version of the state motto beneath the shield is "We Dare Defend Our Rights."

The square state flag is based on the standard flown when Alabama was part of the Confederacy. The plain white field is decorated by the red cross of St. Andrew.

ALASKA

As is evident in the above emblem, seal hunting and mining were the principal pursuits of Alaska during its district status prior to 1912.

Except for modifications in the inscription that were made when Alaska attained statehood in 1958, the present seal is similar to that when Alaska became a territory in 1912.

The Northern Lights, a striking phenomenon in the Alaskan skies, are seen in the background. Snow-clad mountain peaks surround a harbor with several vessels near a mining town; dimly visible in the water are some seals. In the foreground of the design are forests and an agricultural scene.

The blue flag with gold stars is based upon a design devised in 1926 by an Indian schoolboy, Benjamin Benson. Its blue field represents the Alaskan sky and the forget-me-not, Alaska's official flower. The gold typifies the wealth believed to lie hidden in the earth. The seven stars at the left bottom, arranged in the form of the Big Dipper or Great Bear constellation, symbolize strength. The North Star in the upper right corner represents Alaska as the most northerly state of the Union.

ARIZONA

The shield in the seal shows Arizona's rugged mountains rising behind symbols of the state's resources—irrigated fields, grazing cattle, a reservoir, and a dam. The miner standing in front of a quartz mill is a reminder of the state's rich mineral resources.

Above the shield is the state's motto—"Ditat Deus" (God Enriches). The 1912 date is the year in which Arizona, previously a territory since 1863, became the Union's forty-eighth state.

The flag's copper-colored star stands for Arizona's most important mineral. Above the star are seven red and six gold rays representing the original states of the Union. The colors of the rays are those of the banners carried by the Spanish explorers under Coronado when he discovered the region. The lower portion of the flag is deep blue.

ARKANSAS

Essential elements of the territorial seal seen above are evident in the state seal showing an eagle flanked by the angel of mercy and the sword of justice. The goddess of liberty near the eagle is encircled by thirteen stars representing the first thirteen states.

The claws of the eagle hold an olive branch and arrows symbolizing peace and defense. In the bird's beak is a scroll with the motto, "Regnat Populus" (The People Rule).

The shield signifies that Arkansas depends upon its own resources, represented by a steamboat, a beehive, and a sheaf of wheat.

The white diamond design in the red flag symbolizes Arkansas' diamond resources. The twenty-five white stars in the blue borders of the diamond commemorate the fact that Arkansas was the twenty-fifth state to join the Union. The blue star above the state's name symbolizes Arkansas' membership in the Confederacy during the Civil War. The three blue stars below the state's name represent Arkansas' ties to France, Spain, and the United States; these stars also signify that Arkansas was the third state carved from the Louisiana Purchase of 1803.

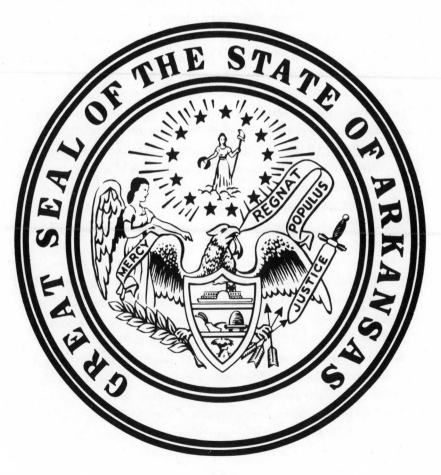

CALIFORNIA

Adopted in 1849, a year before California was admitted into the Union, the seal shows Minerva, Roman goddess of wisdom, sitting near a grizzly bear, the state animal. (Minerva, like California, was born an adult; California never experienced probationary status as a territory.)

In the background are peaks of the Sierra Nevada Mountains, representative of the several ranges which divide the state. Vessels in the harbor indicate the importance of California shipping. In the foreground are a miner digging for gold (a gold rush was under way when the seal was devised), a cluster of grapes, and wheat symbolizing the states mineral and agricultural resources. The stars at the top show that California was the thirty-first state. The adjoining Greek motto "Eureka" means "I have found it."

The state flag is patterned after a flag flown by a group of settlers who revolted against Mexican rule in California on June 14, 1846. It depicts a brown grizzly bear against a white background. A red stripe runs along the lower portion and a red star appears in the upper left hand corner. The word "California Republic," beneath the bear on a green plot, are a reminder of the period from 1822 to 1825 when California was completely independent.

Improvised with a yard-wide strip of homespun cotton, a red flannel shirt and a can of brown paint, the original flag was raised on a staff from which the Mexican flag had been removed. According to tradition, William Todd, a nephew of Mrs. Abraham Lincoln, painted the star in the flag's corner in memory of "the late Republic of Texas."

The government of the Bear Flag men, which extended over a part of southern California, was short-lived. On July 7, 1846, naval forces under Commodore John Sloat landed at Monterey, raised the Stars and Stripes, and proclaimed California a United States conquest.

COLORADO

Dominant elements in the seal, authorized a year after Colorado attained statehood in 1876, are the "seeing eye" of Providence (adopted from the reverse side of the Great Seal of the United States), a bundle of fasces symbolizing the power of God and the people's justice, and a shield with several peaks representing the Great Rockies and mining tools. The Latin motto "Nil Sine Numine" means "Nothing Without Providence."

The colors of the flag's stripes are blue over white over blue. The large red C extending into the stripes has a dual meaning; it represents both Colorado and Centennial; the state was admitted into the Union in 1876, a hundred years after the Declaration of Independence. A golden ball in the center of the C signifies gold deposits and the warming sun. The white stripe symbolizes silver resources and mountain snows; the blue stands for the color of the sky. The red is a heraldic pun; the state's name is derived from the Spanish word for that color.

Some authorities contend that the colors of the flag were originally inspired by the blue, gold, and white of the columbine, Colorado's official flower.

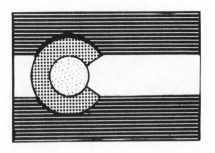

In matters
of greater
consequence
which concern
the
common God
&

General Council

Chosen by all to

transact bvsinesses
er
conceive vnd

which concern all
favor
to
rvle & most

most svitable

safe for relief
of the whole.

Thomas Hooker

CONNECTICUT

Imbedded in the floor of the Connecticut State Library is a collection of four seals. At the lower left of the photo is the colony's first seal, adopted in 1784 and still in use. At the top of this page (left) is a replica of the seal seen in the photo's upper right hand corner. This seal, used between 1662 and 1784, shows the hand of God blessing a vineyard of fifteen vines. The accompanying words, meaning "He who transplanted still sustains," has remained the state's official motto, as is evident in the present coat of arms (right side at the top of this page) and seal. The latter, unaltered since 1784, has three vines believed to represent the state's first three towns; the Latin words in the rim mean "Seal of the Commonwealth of Connecticut."

A nearly square blue flag displays the coat of arms.

33

DELAWARE

The farmer and the rifleman represent the early responsibilities of the people of Delaware—productive work and defense of rights.

The shield displays an ear of Indian corn and a sheaf of wheat (symbols from William Penn's seal) and an ox. The state motto in the scroll, "Liberty and Independence," is a reminder that Delaware was the first state to ratify the nation's Constitution.

The dates in the rim around the seal refer to the years in which the seal was adopted (1793) and modified.

The central motif of the state's blue flag is the design of the seal displayed on a buff-colored background—the colors of the uniforms worn by Revolutionary War soldiers who earned for Delaware the nickname "The Blue Hen State" because their valor was comparable to that of fighting cocks. The date on which Delaware became the first ratifier of the Constitution appears in white letters.

DECEMBER 7, 1787

FLORIDA

The Territory of Florida seal shows an American eagle with outspread wings resting on a bed of clouds. In the right talon of the eagle are three arrows, in the left an olive branch. Above the eagle is a semi-circle of thirteen stars.

In 1846, the year after Florida's admission into the Union, a new seal, showing an outline map of the state, was adopted. On an island in the lower left are several palm trees and an oak under which sits a woman with one hand outstretched toward the Gulf of Mexico and the other holding a pike on which rests a liberty cap. Nearby are casks and a variety of flowering shrubs. On the water are four ships—a three-masted square rigger under full sail, another under jibs and topsails, a schooner, and a fishing vessel. This seal remained in use until it was supplanted by the present seal in 1868, when the state was readmitted into the Union.

Like its predecessor, the current seal includes the state's unofficial motto "In God We Trust." On a sandy spit an Indian woman representing the tribes that originally inhabited the area is seen strewing some of the abundant flowers for which Florida is noted. The state tree, a tall palm—symbol of victory, justice and honor—rises on a sandy shore. A steamboat approaching the harbor symbolizes commercial growth; the setting sun behind the distant hills stands for the state's glory and splendor.

Florida's flag has red bars crossed on a white field (a design taken from the banner flown during Florida's ties with the Confederacy). The state seal is centered where the bars meet. (Legend has it that the red bars were added in 1889 so as to avoid resemblance to a flag of truce when absence of a breeze did not disclose the seal).

37

GEORGIA

Silk worms are on a mulberry leaf in the first seal, adopted by "trustees" who in 1733 founded a colony named in honor of King George II. A primary purpose of the colony was to provide a haven for debtors who agreed to plant mulberry trees needed for British silks. Hence the Latin motto meaning "Not For Ourselves, But For Others." On the reverse side of the seal are figures symbolizing liberty, prosperity, and industry; the accompanying inscription, "Colonia Georgia Aug." (Augeat) stand for "May the Georgia Colony Flourish." When the colony became a royal province in 1753 the front of its seal bore a symbolic representation of the settlers offering a skein of silk to King George II, whose coat of arms is depicted on this seal's reverse side.

The present seal, virtually unchanged since 1799, commemorates Georgia's role as a signer of the Declaration of Independence and the Constitution. In the center are pillars representing the principal branches of state government—legislative, judicial, and executive.

A blue band at the flag's left side bears a blue and white version of the state seal. The crossed bars of blue with twelve white stars surrounded by a red field are derived from the Confederate flag.

38

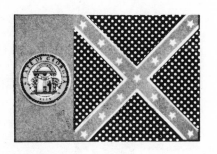

HAWAII

Essentially similar to Hawaii's earlier territorial, republic, and royal seals, the present seal was adopted in 1959 when Hawaii became the fiftieth state. The central feature of the seal is a shield derived from the arms of King Kamehameha I, who united the Hawaiian islands in the 18th century. In the shield are stripes from the state's flag and tabu sticks symbolizing a chief's power.

Standing on scrolls adjoining the shield are Kamahameha and a goddess of liberty holding the state flag. Below them a phoenix rises amid clusters of taro leaves, banana foliage, and sprays of maidenhair fern. The year of Hawaii's statehood appears between rays of the sun. Hawaii's motto (The Life of the Land is Preserved in Righteousness) is in the seal's outer circle.

Facing each other in the coat of arms of the Kingdom of Hawaii seen above are Kamanawa and Kameeiamoku wearing feather cloaks; these warrior twins were tribal chiefs who supported King Kamehameha in his efforts to unite the Hawaiian islands. The motto at the bottom, like that in the present seal, was devised by King Kamehameha III in 1843, when Hawaii's sovereignty was restored.

Hawaii's banner is the only American flag that has flown over a kingdom, a territory, a republic, and finally a state. Its history reaches back to the time when Hawaii was known as the Sandwich Islands, so named in 1778 by Captain James Cook in honor of the British First Lord of the Admiralty. During a visit to the islands in 1793 Captain George Vancouver gave King Kamehameha a Union Jack which subsequently took on both British and American characteristics. The latter are evident in the eight alternately white, red, and blue stripes representing each of Hawaii's islands. The canton at the left is a replica of the Union Jack.

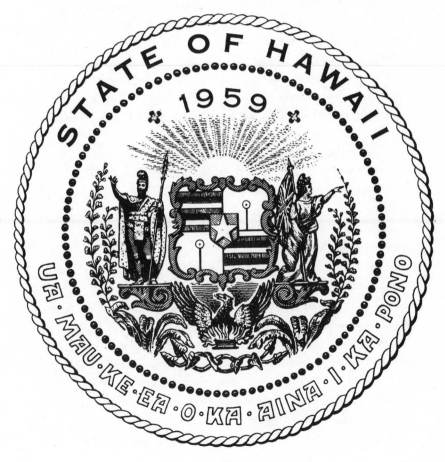

IDAHO

The only state seal designed by a woman (Emma Edwards, the daughter of Idaho's first governor), this seal, adopted in 1891, a year after Idaho became the last state to be carved out of the Oregon territory, emphasizes frontier life. An elk typifying local wildlife peers over a shield depicting the forested shores of the Snake River. Near the female figure is a mixture of wheat and syringa, the state flower. The state's motto "Esto Perpetua" means "It is Forever."

The female figure at the seal's left side represents not only justice and freedom but also the willingness of women to shoulder responsibility. In an article about the seal written by Miss Edwards she explained:

"My father said to me: 'Women are going to do great things; women will be given power . . . So I determined that in my seal there should be a woman as well as a man. In stature she should be almost, but not quite the equal of the man, so that she might still look up to him; she should be of heroic build. . .

"The syringa grows wild in our Idaho mountains, where its roots bravely cling to rocks and jutting crags.

"The man typifies the courage, the strength and the keen, clear judgment which have wrested our beautiful state from the roving savage and from the barrenness imposed by nature, and which have unbarred the gates guarding her mighty resources. He is shown as a miner in honor of those sturdy pioneers through whose instrumentality Idaho took her first steps in development."

A blue banner bearing the seal constitutes the state flag.

ILLINOIS

The first of the seals used for official documents in what is now Illinois was known as "The Seal of the Territory of the U.S.N.W. of the Ohio River."

In 1800, when Indiana Territory (including Illinois), was created, the seal of the Northwest Territory was adopted; nine years later, when Illinois Territory came into existence, its seal was almost an exact copy of the Great Seal of the U.S.

When Illinois gained statehood in 1818 its seal was another duplicate of the U. S. seal, but it differed from the preceding seal in that the eagle held a scroll in its beak on which were the words of the state motto, "State Sovereignty, National Union." As previously, the eagle held arrows in one talon, an olive branch in the other.

In 1868 the present seal was adopted. It shows an American eagle perched on a rock bearing the dates 1818 and 1868. The bird holds a shield based on the Stars and Stripes of the original thirteen states and carries in its beak a scroll bearing the state motto. Beneath the shield is an olive branch for peace.

In 1915 Illinois adopted the present gold-edged flag. Centered in the field is a replica of the eagle carrying in its beak a red motto scroll with gold lettering. The shield on the eagle's breast is in red, white, and blue.

INDIANA

Like the territorial seal, the present seal, authorized in
1963, is slightly different from the design of the seal speci-
fied when Indiana became a state in 1816: "A forest and a
woodman felling a tree, a buffalo leaving the forest and
fleeing through the plain to a distant forest, and the sun setting in the west." The mountains in the background have
been variously explained as the Alleghenies, the Rockies
and "the hills lying east of Vincennes."

The almost square blue and gold state flag was adopted in
1917 as part of the commemoration of the state's centennial.
The flaming torch in the center stands for liberty and enlightenment; the rays symbolize far-reaching influence. The outer
circle of stars represents the original thirteen states; the
inner circle of stars stands for the five states next admitted to
the Union. The slightly larger star above the torch represents
Indiana, the nineteenth state. Prior to 1917 the national
flag served as the state flag.

IOWA

Indicative of Iowa's transition to statehood in 1846 is the marked difference between its territorial and state seals. In regard to the significance of the former, Territory Secretary William Conway explained that the Indian arrow held in the eagle's beak and the unstrung bow clutched in its talons expressed an idea "well calculated to cause the heart to beat high with the pulsations of conscious superiority" as well as "appeal to our manly sensibilities in contemplating the dreary destiny of a declining race." Conway also felt that the design would "admonish us of the importance of improving . . . the [Indian's] inheritance which it was their peculiar misfortune to undervalue and neglect."

When Iowa became the twenty-eighth state it adopted a seal testifying to the industriousness and patriotism of the early settlers. The scroll held in the eagle's beak bears the state motto, "Our Liberties We Prize and Our Rights We Will Maintain." A citizen soldier is seen standing guard near a wheat field, farming implements, and a log cabin. In the background the steamboat "Iowa" is heading upstream on the Mississippi River.

The seal's motto bearing eagle is centered in the blue, white, and red colors of the state flag.

KANSAS

Beneath the state's Latin motto, "Ad Astro Per Aspera" (To the Stars Through Difficulties), are thirty-four stars representing the states in the Union when Kansas achieved statehood in 1861. The "difficulties" refer to the slavery question which for many years prevented the Kansas territory from becoming a state.

The buffalo and the Indian, the oxen and the prairie schooners, the cabin and the plowman tell the early story of Kansas in sequence. The hills identify terrain near Fort Riley.

Centered in the blue field of the Kansas flag is the seal topped by the state flower, a red and yellow sunflower. The adjoining bar signifies the Louisiana Purchase including land that become Kansas. In 1963 the name of the state was incorporated in the flag.

KENTUCKY

Brotherhood is the predominant sentiment in the seal adopted in 1792, when Kentucky became the fifteenth state. Two men shaking hands in the center of the design are surrounded by a scroll bearing the state's motto, "United We Stand, Divided We Fall." This motto, in the opinion of flag historian Whitney Smith, is a paraphrase of a refrain in a popular Revolutionary War song ("Then join in hand, brave Americans all, By uniting we stand, by dividing we fall"). "United We Stand, Divided We Fall" is also the motto of Missouri, another border state that remained loyal to the Union during the Civil War.

Since 1962 another version of the seal shows a frontiersman dressed in buckskin of frontier days, clasping the right hand of a Kentuckian wearing a formal frock coat and striped pants. (This version has been authorized for use on the flag.)

In 1962 Kentucky adopted as its official flag a modified version of an earlier blue banner. A wreath of goldenrod, the state flower, forms a yellow garland below the centered state seal. "Commonwealth of Kentucky" appears in gold letters. An unusual feature of flag regulations requires that a replica of the state bird, the cardinal, appear at the top of flag poles.

LOUISIANA

The design of the state's seal, traceable to 1804, shows a mother pelican (known as a "pelican in her piety" or "a pelican vulning herself") with wings outstretched as she feeds baby birds in their nest. Self-sacrifice is symbolized by the fact that the mother's beak is tearing at her breast in order to sustain her young. (The Eastern Brown Pelican is Louisiana's official bird.) The words of the state motto, "Union Justice, Confidence," surround the birds.

In 1912, the centennial year of statehood, Louisiana adopted a blue flag bearing the gold and white pelican symbol with the motto displayed on a white scroll underneath.

Many flags have flown over Louisiana. Until 1762 the golden lilies of the French kings, the yellow fleur-de-lis flecked on a white shield, waved from the capitol at New Orleans. It was replaced by the red, white, and yellow flag of Spain, with golden castles and red lions on a white field; in 1785 this flag was changed by inclusion of bars representing the province of Aragon. During the period when portions of Florida belonged to England flags bearing the crosses of St. George and St. Andrew were flown.

There are also nineteenth century references to a "Pelican Flag." In 1862 such a flag was removed from the State House in Baton Rouge, when Admiral Farragut captured the city during the Civil War.

MAINE

Previously a part of Massachusetts, Maine adopted its distinctive seal when it became the twenty-third state of the Union in 1820. Typical early inhabitants, a fisherman and a farmer, adjoin a shield featuring a tall pine tree. During the eighteenth and nineteenth centuries tall white pines, which grow as high as two hundred feet, were used for ship masts and provided the state's most important source of income. A recumbent moose lies under the branches of the pine tree in the seal. A pine cone is the state floral emblem. Maine's nickname, "Pine Tree State," is an allusion to its evergreen forests. Above the shield is the North Star marking Maine's location as the most northern of the east coast states. The state motto, "Dirigo," means "I guide" or "I direct."

A blue flag includes the design of the state seal. During the Revolutionary War a "Pine-tree Flag" was one of the banners flown in New England.

MARYLAND

Seventh state to ratify the Constitution, Maryland uses as its official emblem a seal based on the coat of arms of its founder, Lord Baltimore.

Encircling the front of the seal is a border including a Latin line from the Psalms ("As with a shield you will crown us by your good will"), an allusion to the colony's ideal of religious freedom.

A farmer dressed in homespun and a fisherman symbolize Lord Baltimore's estates in Maryland and Avalon, a Newfoundland colony. They are holding a shield bearing the arms of the Calverts and Crosslands, Lord Baltimore's two families. Underneath is a scroll with the Calvert motto ("Deeds are masculine, words feminine.")

The seal's reverse side shows Lord Baltimore as a medieval knight on a horse with the family banner, encircled by a Latin inscription meaning "Carolus, Absolute Lord of Maryland and Avalon, Baron of Baltimore."

The flag includes the arms of Lord Baltimore's families. Two quarters carry the Calvert arms, vertical black and gold bars crossed by a diagonal of the same colors reversed; the other segments consist of the Crossland arms, a red and white cross on a quartered red and white field.

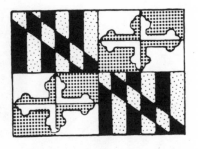

59

MASSACHUSETTS

Named for the Indian tribe living on the shores of Plymouth Bay when the Pilgrim settlers arrived in 1620, Massachusetts has a seal with elements dating from that period.

At the top of this page is the seal of the Massachusetts Bay Colony under the charter granted by Charles I in 1629. During the pre-Revolutionary era the royal coat of arms of England was the seal of the Province of Massachusetts.

In 1775, following hostilities with England, Massachusetts adopted the seal showing a rebellious colonist holding a Magna Charta. The Latin words within the inner circle (meaning "By the Sword We Seek Peace, But Peace Only Under Liberty") have been the state's motto down through the years. The adjoining seal at the bottom was adopted by Massachusetts in 1780.

In 1898 the present seal (seen on the next page) was authorized. As in the 1780 seal, the central figure is an Indian holding a bow and an arrow pointed downward to symbolize peace. Above his right shoulder a five-pointed star represents Massachusetts as one of the original states. The crest is a sturdy arm grasping a broadsword. The lettering in the scroll surrounding the shield has the motto adopted in 1775.

Both sides of the flag have white backgrounds. The front side carries the seal's design; the reverse side bears a blue shield displaying a pine tree symbolizing the importance of forests in the early life of the state.

MICHIGAN

Above are a symbol of early French dominion in Michigan and the first territorial seal.

The only seal designed by a man who ran for President of the United States, Michigan's seal is based in part on the coat of arms of the Hudson Bay Colony. Two animals native to both Michigan and adjoining Canada, an elk (left) and a moose (right), are reminders of the region's early wildlife and fur trade. Lewis Cass, governor of the Michigan territory (1813-1831) and presidential nominee of the Democratic Party in 1848, devised the seal when Michigan was admitted to the Union in 1835.

The word "Tuebor," meaning "I will defend," refers to the northern frontier position of Michigan. The small shield shows the rising sun casting its rays over a lake toward a frontiersman standing on a peninsula. The upraised right hand of the frontiersman symbolizes peace: his gunpowder horn indicates preparedness to defend the state and Union.

The Latin inscription below means "If you seek a pleasant peninsula, look about you." This evidently refers to Michigan's lower peninsula. In 1837 the upper peninsula became part of Michigan in compensation for the loss of a strip of land on the southern border obtained by Ohio when Congress recognized Michigan as a state.

A blue flag bearing the seal was adopted in 1911.

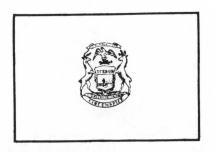

MINNESOTA

Due to what is believed to be a mistake, the territorial seal depicts an armed Indian riding eastward while a farmer plowed in the opposite direction. Many settlers ridiculed this seal because it seemed to show a scared settler watching a frightened Indian gallop away underneath a Latin motto meaning "I want to see what is beyond."

When Minnesota became a state in 1858 the seal was revised to show the settler plowing eastward and a displaced Sioux Indian riding off to the west. Moreover, the motto was changed to "L'Etoile du Nord" (The Star of the North), a reminder that this area was first discovered by French explorers. The scenic Falls of St. Anthony are seen in the background.

The blue flag shows the state seal and nineteen stars; Minnesota was the nineteenth state to enter the Union after the formation of the latter by the thirteen original colonies. Dates on the flag are 1858 (statehood), 1819 (the erection of Fort St. Anthony (later named Fort Snelling), and 1893 (the year the present flag was adopted). The dates and the motto are lettered in red.

MISSISSIPPI

The seal shows the familiar American eagle bearing a shield on its breast and clutching a palm branch in one claw and a quiver of arrows in the other.

The eagle also appears on the state coat of arms traceable back to 1798. Below the shield are branches of the cotton plant, the state's leading crop. A ribbon carries the state's motto "Virtute et Armis" (By Virtue and Arms).

The Mississippi flag represents the state's ties to the Confederacy and the United States. The design at the upper left is the Confederate battle flag; the colors are those of the national flag.

During the Civil War, Mississippi, like other members of the Southern Confederacy, accepted the national seal and flag of the Confederacy. The very first flag had a blue union with a circle of stars representing the states in the Confederacy. It had two red stripes and a white bar of equal width. Better known was the Confederate battle flag— a square red field upon which a St. Andrew's cross of blue extended diagonally from corner to corner. Five white stars for each Confederate state were in the cross. In time the Confederate flag was modified to include the battle flag in the corner.

MISSOURI

The stars on the seal proclaim that Missouri (which takes its name from the river whose Indiana name means "people of the long canoes") became the twenty-fourth state in 1821.

Two grizzly bears, symbol of the state's ability to support itself and the Union, hold a circular shield whose border carries the motto "United We Stand, Divided We Fall." The Latin at the bottom ("Salus Populi Suprema Lex Esto") stands for "The Welfare of the People Shall Be the Supreme Law."

The shield's right side displays the arms of the United States, while the other half includes symbols of Missouri: a bear for strength and courage and a crescent moon. The latter, heraldic sign of a second son, signifies that Missouri was the second state created from the Louisiana Purchase.

Twenty-three stars above the helmet of sovereignty stand for the states which preceded Missouri in the Union. The Roman numerals at the bottom mark the date of the state constitution, 1823.

The official flag is a red, white, and blue tricolor with the state arms encircled by a blue ring carrying twenty-four white stars. The blue stripe represents vigilance, permanency, and justice; white symbolizes purity.

MONTANA

Based upon a design used in Montana's territorial seal, the present seal, adopted in 1889 (when Montana was admitted to statehood), focuses on the state's scenic splendors. The farm and mining tools represent agriculture and mineral resources. The Great Falls of the Missouri River and rugged mountain peaks are seen in the background. The state's Spanish motto, "Oro Y Plata" (Gold and Silver), appears on a scroll at the base.

The flag consists of a blue field displaying the state seal minus the latter's encircling inscription.

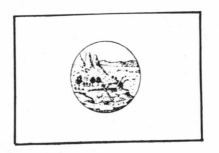

NEBRASKA

Above is Nebraska's territorial seal. The principal resources of the state are evident in the seal adopted in 1867, when statehood was attained. The blacksmith in the foreground typifies the mechanical arts. Agriculture is represented by sheaves of wheat, stalks of corn, and the cabin of a pioneer settler. The steamboat on the Missouri River and the train remind us of the importance of transportation in the growth of the state. The Rocky Mountains are seen near the state's motto, "Equality before the law." The post-Civil War struggle for civil rights was in process when this motto was adopted but, according to the seal's designer, the motto related to the right of each settler to a tract of public land in the state.

The state's flag is a dark blue banner with Nebraska's gold and silver seal in the center.

NEVADA

Appropriately enough, loyalty to the Union is emphasized in the seal mineral-rich Nevada adopted when it was granted territorial status shortly after the Civil War broke out. The motto beneath the miner, "Volens et Potens" (Willing and Able), signifies both loyalty and the resources to sustain it. In 1864, when adoption of the 13th and 14th amendments to the Constitution required the vote of an additional loyal state, the territory was hurriedly admitted into the Union at the urging of President Lincoln.

Slightly different from the original state seal, the present seal pictures Nevada's mining and agricultural resources. Towering mountains provide a setting for a quartz mill, a mine tunnel, a trainload of ore, a sheaf of wheat, and farm equipment. The rim of the seal includes thirty-six stars, an allusion to Nevada's admission into the Union as the thirty-sixth state, and the state's motto, "All For Our Country."

In the upper left-hand corner of the blue flag is a silver star surrounded by a wreath of sagebrush, the state flower. The words "Battle Born" set in a gold scroll, are a reminder that Nevada entered the Union during the Civil War. Interspersing the points of the star are letters spelling out the state's name.

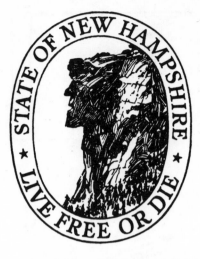

NEW HAMPSHIRE

In addition to its seal, New Hampshire has a state emblem depicting the picturesque "Old Man of the Mountains," a famous rock formation at Franconia Notch about which Daniel Webster said God shaped it to signify the character of New Hampshire men. This emblem bears the state motto, "Live Free Or Die," a reminder that New Hampshire was the first colony to establish a government independent of Great Britain. Its 1776 seal depicts a fish, a pine tree, and five bound arrows near the motto "Vis Unita Fortior" (Strength United Is Stronger). The arrows symbolize New Hampshire's counties. A subsequent state seal focused on a shipyard scene was replaced in 1784 by a seal that has remained essentially unchanged since then. The central feature is a ship (believed to be the Revolutionary War frigate "Raleigh" built at Portsmouth) surrounded by the laurel wreath of victory. 1776 is the year when New Hampshire's constitution was adopted.

The blue flag, only slightly different from a banner flown since 1792, displays the seal surrounded by an outer wreath of golden laurel leaves interspersed with nine stars signifying that New Hampshire was the ninth state to ratify the nation's constitution.

NEW JERSEY

Above is the seal of East Jersey prior to its amalgamation with West Jersey during the Revolutionary War years.

The state seal's goddess of Liberty is holding a staff with a Phrygian cap symbolizing freedom; on the right is Ceres, the goddess of vegetation holding a cornucopia, the symbol of prosperity and abundance. The shield bears several plows emphasizing the importance of farming in New Jersey's history. Below the goddesses is a scroll carrying the state motto "Liberty and Prosperity" and the historic date 1776.

The horse's head resting on an earl's helmet represents speed, strength, and usefulness to commerce. The helmet is a symbol of sovereignty.

The state flag displays the design of the seal on a field of buff, a color derived from the facings of uniforms of New Jersey's Revolutionary soldiers.

NEW MEXICO

The wings of the American eagle in the state seal shield a Mexican eagle representing the taking over of New Mexico by the United States. Although the latter assumed sovereignty over the territory after the war with Mexico in 1847, New Mexico did not become the forty-seventh state until 1912, a year before the seal was adopted. (Reproduced above at left is the New Mexico territorial seal).

The talons of the American eagle grasp the arrows of war. The smaller eagle with its snake and cactus is derived from the Mexican coat of arms. The adjoining scroll bears the state motto "Crescit Eundo" (It Grows As It Goes).

The flag tells of New Mexico's Indian and Spanish origins. The red sun of the Zia Indian pueblo in the center of the yellow flag represents "perfect friendship among united cultures." Red and yellow were also the colors of King Ferdinand and Queen Isabella, rulers of Spain; those colors were in the flag carried by Coronado when he entered Mexico in 1540.

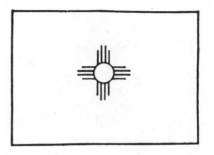

Crescit Eundo

NEW YORK

During the Dutch occupation period, when New York was known as New Netherlands, the seal consisted of a beaver, symbol of the fur trade, on a shield enclosed by wampum, symbol of wealth. The earl's crown signified that the territory was a province of The Netherlands.

Indicative of the growing importance of agriculture are the windmills and barrels of flour seen in the 1686 British seal. An additional seal, authorized in 1691, shows Indians offering gifts to King William and Queen Mary.

The present seal includes symbols of New York's Dutch and English heritage. The shield depicts a Hudson River scene with white-sailed ships in a harbor near mountains. The sun rising in the background has been traced to the coats of arms of Jonas Bronck, a Dutchman for whom the Bronx derived its name, and the English Duke of York, who gained control of the colony in 1664. At the feet of Liberty (left of the shield) is a crown symbolizing the overthrow of royal rule. Justice holds a sword and scales.

The state's motto "Excelsior" (Ever Upward) appears in the scroll beneath the shield. Tradition has it that the eagle perched on a globe signifies "Westward the course of empire takes its way."

In 1901 New York officially replaced the buff of its flag (taken from the color of Revolutionary uniform facings) with a deep blue.

NORTH CAROLINA

In 1663, when King Charles II granted to eight lords proprietors an area of land including what is now North Carolina, their seal (seen above) bore a coat of arms showing a stag at the crest, an Indian couple, and crossed cornucopias symbolizing the wealth expected from the territory. Later, when North Carolina became a royal colony, the royal arms were on the front side of the seal. A map of the area served as the background of the seal's reverse side showing a cornucopia being presented to King George by the deity of Plenty; behind his throne stood Liberty.

Although somewhat different from the seal adopted by North Carolina after it declared its independence from England, the present seal, authorized in 1893, also includes deities representing Liberty and Plenty. The former (left) is holding a scroll inscribed Constitution and a pole with a liberty cap. Plenty is seated near a cornucopia with fruits and vegetables symbolic of the state's resources; in her right hand are stalks of grain.

May 20, 1775, the date above the deities, is the day on which North Carolina declared its independence from England. The state's motto—"Esse Quam Videri" (To Be Rather Than To Seem To Be)—is at the bottom of the seal.

The state's flag has red and white stripes. In the blue band at the left is a white star; above and below are yellow scrolls with the dates May 20, 1775 and April 12, 1776. On the latter date North Carolina's delegates to the Continental Congress were empowered to join other colonists in voting for independence.

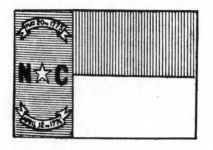

NORTH DAKOTA

Based on the Dakota Territory seal (see South Dakota), the state seal depicts a Sioux Indian pursuing a buffalo and symbols of agriculture and industry.

The forty-two stars in the seal represent the states in the Union when North Dakota attained statehood in 1889. The motto of the state, "Liberty and union, now and forever, one and inseparable," adjoins the stars.

A Sioux arrowhead, based upon a motif taken from the coats of arms of Meriwether Lewis, pioneer explorer of the northwest, constitutes the shield of the state's coat of arms (above). The three stars denote the trinity of government—legislative, executive, and judicial. Each star has the heraldic value of thirteen signifying the thirteen original colonies of the U. S. and the cumulative numerical value of the three stars indicates that North Dakota was the thirty-ninth state admitted into the Union. The stars also allude to the history of the territory under three foreign flags. Three stars were borne upon the coats of arms of Meriwether Lewis and Lord Selkirk; the latter headed the first permanent settlement in the state. The crest, based upon a motif taken from the state seal, signifies that the Sioux Indians were mighty warriors.

The fleur-de-lis alludes to LaVerendyre, a French explorer who was the first white man to visit the territory.

A stylized version of the American eagle, adapted from the banner flown by the Dakota Territorial Guard, appears in the center of the state's blue flag. The stars stand for the thirteen original states.

OHIO

In 1803 the state's first legislature adopted a law specifying the seal's original design: "On the right side, near the bottom, a sheaf of wheat and on the left a bundle of arrows, both standing erect; in the background, and rising above the sheaf and bundle of arrows a mountain, over which shall appear the rising sun." Two years later, however, the legislature inadvertently repealed the original act. Subsequently different seals came into usage.

In 1866 a Republican-controlled legislature passed a law creating a new seal utilizing the 1803 symbols but also including the motto "Imperium in Imperio" (An empire within an empire.) The latter displeased Democrats who considered the motto imperialistic. An 1866 law provided for a seal similar to that of 1803. This law governed the seal's design until the present version, adopted in 1967.

For many years historians assumed the mountains represented the Alleghenies over which a rising sun was shining on Ohio's western lands but it is now believed the design was inspired by the spectacle of Mt. Logan seen by Thomas Worthington, one of Ohio's first senators, Edward Tiffin, first governor, and William Creighton, first secretary of state.

The symbolism of the pennant-shaped flag is in part fanciful. The triangles formed by the flag's main lines allude to hills and valleys and the red and white stripes stand for roads and waterways. White stars representing the thirteen original states are grouped about a red circle symbolizing the original Northwest Territory. The fact that Ohio was the seventeenth state admitted into the Union is indicated by additional stars at the right side of the triangle's blue field. The white circle surrounding the red center not only represents the initial letter of Ohio but is also suggestive of its nickname "Buckeye State."

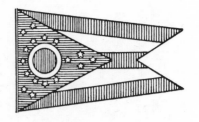

OKLAHOMA

In the center of the seal's large star is a three-figured symbol of the frontiersman, the Indian, and justice. Above them is the state motto meaning "Labor Conquers All."

Symbols of Oklahoma's Indian tribes appear in the rays of the large star. In the upper left ray is a seven-pointed star bearing a wreath of oak leaves, symbol of the Cherokee Nation. The upward ray in the center depicts an Indian warrior with bow and shield, ancient seal of the Chicasaw Nation. The emblem of the Choctaw Nation in the upper right ray is comprised of a tomahawk, a bow and three crossed arrows. The Seminole Nation is represented by an Indian hunter paddling a canoe in the lower right ray. In the lower left ray is the symbol of the Creek Nation, depicted by a sheaf of wheat and a plow.

Surrounding the central star are forty-five small stars, representing the states that comprised the Union at the time Oklahoma attained statehood in 1907.

The center of the flag shows an Osage warrior's buckskin shield, decorated with pendant eagle feathers. Across the face of the shield runs the red man's Calumet, or pipe of peace, crossed with the white man's peace symbol, the olive branch. The field of the flag is the blue of Oklahoma skies; the shield is light tan, with white feathers tipped with brown; the small crosses are tan and the Calumet has a red bowl; the pale yellow ivory stem has a red feather tassel. The olive branch is gray green and the word "Oklahoma" is pure white. The blue field signifies loyalty. The shield implies defense. The tan crosses, Indian sign for stars, indicate ideals.

90

OREGON

Prior to the present seal Oregon had as many as nine different seals of uncertain status and duration. The first seal, adopted by a provisional government in 1843, featured a salmon and several sheaves of wheat.

During the territorial years 1848-58 variations of a new seal included an Indian, a beaver, and the motto "Alis Volat Propriis" (I Fly With My Own Wings). The motto reflected the sentiment that "Oregon has flown so far by her own wings . . . and can wing her way to new heights."

Essentials of the present seal are conspicious in early state seals, some erroneously containing the date 1857, two years before statehood was actually reached.

The present seal is primarily a tribute to the state's pioneer settlers—especially evident in the agricultural symbols and the covered wagon drawn by oxen. The end of British influence in Oregon is signified in the Pacific Ocean background showing a British man-of-war departing and an American merchant ship arriving. Also evident in the crowned heart-shaped shield are mountains, forest trees, and an elk. The thirty-three stars around the shield stand for the fact that Oregon was the thirty-third state to join the Union.

The seal's shield appears in gold on the front of the state's blue flag. On the reverse side a beaver, important for its furs in the commerce of Oregon's pioneer days and a reminder of the state's nickname, is also depicted in gold.

PENNSYLVANIA

The main difference between the state seal on the next page and the coat of arms (above) is that harnessed horses face each other on each side of the shield in the latter. Underneath the horses is scrollwork entwined with a ribbon bearing the state's long-standing motto.

The three segments of the shield in both the seal and the coat of arms include a white-sailed ship, a plow, and sheaves of wheat. The ship and wheat sheaves derive from an early seal of Philadelphia; the plow came from the Chester County coat of arms under the proprietorship of Quaker William Penn. At the bottom of this page is the seal of the period when Penn was sole proprietor of "Pensilvania."

Perched atop the shield is an eagle epitomizing speed, strength, and bravery. Surrounding the bottom of the shield is a wreath composed of a stalk of corn and an olive branch. (The design on the reverse side of the seal shows Liberty with her sword drawn against the subdued lion of despotism.)

Centered in the state's blue flag is the coat of arms.

94

RHODE ISLAND

The anchor, symbol of hope, is the outstanding feature in both the coat of arms (above) and seal of the State of Rhode Island and Providence Plantations. "Hope" is the official motto.

The date in the present seal is the year when Roger Williams, a radical Puritan banned from the Massachusetts Bay Colony, founded what became Providence, the state's capital city.

The state flag has a gold-edged white field displaying the gold anchor and blue motto scroll surrounded by thirteen gold stars representing the original colonies. White is derived from the color of uniforms worn by Rhode Island's Revolutionary war soldiers.

SOUTH CAROLINA

Both of the representations in the seal symbolize the battle against British forces which took place at Sullivan's Island (later named Fort Moultrie) on June 28, 1776.

The palmetto tree, the kind with which the fort was built, towers over a fallen oak symbolizing the defeated English ships. Attached to the tree are two historic dates—March 26, the day on which South Carolina declared its independence from Britain in 1776 and July 4, national independence day. The twelve spears attached to the palmetto's stem, united by a band inscribed "Quis Separabit" ("Who Will Separate [Them]?"), represent the twelve states which first joined the Union. Under the prostrate oak is a motto meaning "He Has Planted One Better Than the Fallen." The motto in the oval's rim stands for "Prepared in Mind and Resources."

The other portion of the seal shows a figure of Hope (her Latin name "Spes") encircled by the motto "Dum Spiro Spero" ("While I Breathe I Hope"). She is walking over swords and daggers as she holds a laurel branch.

The blue state flag has a silver crescent and a palmetto tree. Both the new moon device and the blue color are derived from the uniforms and cap badges of the South Carolina regiments that fought for independence during the Revolutionary War.

SOUTH DAKOTA

Commerce, industry, and farming are represented in the state's seal. Mineral resources and mining are symbolized by the smelter set against the mountain at the left. "Under God the people rule" is the state's motto. The date at the bottom of the seal is the year in which South Dakota attained statehood. Previously it was part of the Dakota Territory represented by the seal at the top of this page.

The flag has a sky blue field displaying the state seal in black and white surrounded by the name of the state and the nickname "The Sunshine State" in gold.

TENNESSEE

The crude riverboat in the earlier state seal (above) was replaced by a more substantial vessel when the present version of the seal was adopted. Otherwise both seals are similar in calling attention to the state's pride in its agriculture (sheaf of wheat and cotton plant) and commerce (inland water transportation). The Roman numeral XVI notes that Tennessee became the sixteenth state in 1796.

The red, white, and blue flag was inspired by the state's three distinct geographical regions. Three white stars on a white-rimmed blue disk in the center of a red field symbolize each of these regions, grouped in a circle to include unity. The three stars have also been suggested as representing three Presidents who lived in Tennessee (Andrew Jackson, James K. Polk, and Andrew Johnson). At the right side of the flag is a fine white line and a narrow blue bar.

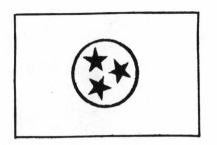

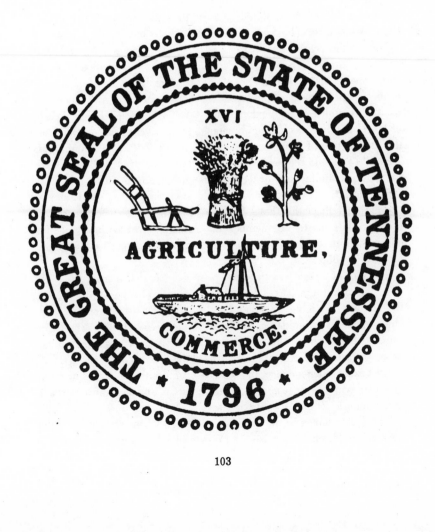

TEXAS

Because of the five-pointed star on its seal and flag, Texas has been nicknamed "The Lone Star State" since statehood in 1845.

During the years when Texas was a Spanish province its seal and flag were those of Spain. Subsequently, after Mexico broke away from Spain, the seal and flag of Texas were those of Mexico. In 1836, when Texas won independence from Mexico and declared itself a republic, it adopted the star symbol encircled by a wreath of laurel and live oak. The only change made in the seal in 1845 was the substitution of "The State of Texas" in place of "The Republic of Texas." The star represents the state; the olive branch, peace; and the live oak, indigenous of Texas, strength and fertility.

The design of the reverse side of the seal, adopted in 1961, shows the national flags that have flown over Texas in the course of its history. The motto "Remember the Alamo" is a reminder of the stirring shout at the battle of San Jancinto during the war with Mexico in 1836.

The flag of Spain was the first to fly over Texas. During the 300-year Spanish reign Texas had several flags. The best-known bore the emblems of King Ferdinand (a red lion on a silver field) and Queen Isabella (a golden castle on a red field). In 1685 France laid claim to Texas when Robert LaSalle planted his country's flag (golden lillies on a field of white) at a fort on the Texas coast. From 1821 until Texas independence in 1836 the predominant flag bore the Mexican symbol—an eagle perched on cactus and holding a serpent in its mouth. (See New Mexico seal).

The Texas star is in the blue bar at the left of the state flag on the next page. The field consists of horizontal white and red stripes.

UTAH

The beehive in the territorial and state seals is derived from the original Mormon name for the state, "Deseret"—honeybee. The sego lilies flanking the beehive in the state seal were chosen as the official flower because the early Mormon settlers subsisted on the bulbs of the plant when food was scarce. The date 1847 refers to the year in which the Mormons completed their trek to Salt Lake City.

The seal, adopted at the time of Utah's statehood in 1896, includes an American eagle symbolizing protection; the national flags indicate loyalty to the Union. "Industry," exemplified by the beehive, is Utah's motto.

The state flag, blue with a gold edge, displays the state seal design surrounded by a golden ring.

VERMONT

The coat of arms (above) depicts a peaceful rural scene characteristic of the state. In the background the thickly-forested Green Mountains, a reminder of Vermont's nickname, surround Lake Champlain. The crest's deer head stands for the state's wildlife. The pine tree branches flanking the bottom of the shield are derived from the insignia worn by Vermont troops in the Battle of Plattsburgh during the War of 1812. "Freedom and Unity" is the state's slogan.

The present seal is a faithful reproduction of the stylized design originally devised in 1779. The fourteen branches of the large pine tree are an allusion to the fact that Vermont became the first new state to join the original thirteen states.

The flag consists of a blue field displaying the coat of arms.

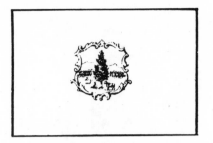

VIRGINIA

The virgin queen crest of the Virginia Company's seal is a tribute to Elizabeth "the Virgin Queen" who reigned during the settlement of Virginia. The front of the seal of the Virginia Council during colonization shows Elizabeth's successor, King James I; the Latin inscription on both sides of the seal means "Seal of the King of Great Britain, France, and Ireland for his Council of Virginia." (England's monarch was also King of parts of France from the time of the Hundred Years War down to the reign of Queen Mary.

Composed of classical Roman figures, the design of the seal adopted after Virginia broke away from England, is credited to George Wythe, a signer of the Declaration of Independence. The front side shows Virtue clad as an Amazon warrior standing triumphantly over a defeated tyrant whose crown lies nearby. "Sic Semper Tyrannis" (Thus Ever to Tyrants) is the state's motto. The reverse of the seal shows Eternity with a globe and phoenix, Liberty holding a staff with a liberty cap, and Ceres, the deity of agriculture, holding an ear of wheat and a cornucopia.

The blue state flag includes the front side of the seal.

110

WASHINGTON

The early hardships of the settlers of Washington are depicted in the territorial seal adopted in 1854. The log cabin, the fir grove, and the prairie schooner represent humble pioneer beginnings while a steamboat and city buildings prefigure anticipated commerce and progress. The woman with an anchor beside her symbolizes hope. The motto "Al-ki," derived from a Chinook Indian expression meaning desire for prosperity, became the state's motto.

In 1889, when Washington joined the union, the territorial seal was discarded in favor of the present design. The likeness of George Washington is said to have been inspired by the familiar postage stamp.

The green field of the flag represents the state's forests.

WEST VIRGINIA

Unchanged since it was adopted in 1863, the seal symbolizes the state's principal pursuits and resources. A farmer and a miner are standing beside an ivy-draped rock bearing the date when West Virginia was admitted to the Union. Lying in front of the rock are a liberty cap and rifles— evidence of the state's determination to adhere to the Union during the Civil War. Inside the seal's border is the state motto, "Montani Semper Liberi" (Mountaineers Are Always Free).

Laurel and oak leaves circle the scene on the seal's reverse side (above) showing some of the state's industries.

In the center of the white state flag is an adaptation of the seal surrounded by a wreath of green and white rhododendron, the state flower.

WISCONSIN

Lead mining, a major Wisconsin industry during the first half of the nineteenth century, and farming are featured in early territorial seals. The capitol in Madison is depicted in the seal at the right.

Labor at sea and on land are represented in the present seal, adopted in 1851. The presence of a sailor and an anchor alludes to the fact that Wisconsin provided manpower for vessels of the nearby Great Lakes. Below the state's motto, "Forward," is a badger, an animal native to the region and the source of the state's nickname. Within the shield's circle is the national motto, "E Pluribus Unum" (One Out of Many) expressing Wisconsin's loyalty to the Union. A cornucopia and a triangular pile of pig iron symbolize the fruits of agriculture and mining. The thirteen stars stand for the original states of the Union.

The seal's design is centered on both sides of the flag, a dark blue banner fringed in gold.

116

WYOMING

The inscription on Wyoming's territorial seal (above) has been variously translated as "Let Arms Yield to the Gown" and "Let Military Authority Give Way to Civil Power."

The female figure in the state seal is an allusion to Wyoming's boast that it was the first area in the United States to grant women the right to vote. This occurred in 1869, the same year in which Wyoming attained territorial status. A year later Esther Morris of South Pass City became the nation's first woman Justice of Peace and in 1924 Nellie Tayloe Ross of Cheyenne became both the state's and the nation's first woman Governor. "Equal Rights," Wyoming's motto, appears on the seal.

The presence of a cowboy and a miner symbolize the principal occupations of the state during the nineteenth century. The Roman numerals on the pedestal refer to the fact that Wyoming became the forty-fourth state in 1890; the lamps on the pillars represent the light of knowledge.

The seal appears in the flag's white silhouette of a buffalo, symbol of the struggle to tame the West. The white border surrounding a dark blue field stand for purity and uprightness; the blue represents the color of the sky and distant mountains as well as virility, justice, and fidelity. The outer red border symbolizes the state's original Indian population and the blood shed by early pioneers.

118

DISTRICT OF COLUMBIA

Appropriately enough, the Capitol, a figure of Justice holding a copy of the Constitution, a statue of George Washington, and an eagle are predominant symbols in the seal of
the District of Columbia. The motto "Justica Omnibus"
(Justice to All) adjoins the date when the seal was adopted
by the District's Legislative Assembly.

The design of the flag's red and white stars and stripes is
said to be derived from the coat of arms of Washington's family.

PUERTO RICO

The seal bespeaks Puerto Rico's ancient Spanish heritage. It is based upon a coat of arms granted by King Ferdinand in 1511. The lamb and the motto represent St. John the Baptist for whom Columbus originally named the island. The yoke and arrows—symbols of affection, unity, and strength—appeared on the personal property of Ferdinand and Queen Isabella. The flags depict the coats of arms of various kingdoms under their reign. The lions and castles represent Leon and Castile, Isabella's hereditary kingdoms; the Crusaders' crosses signify Spanish conquest of the Moors.

The flag, adopted in 1952, bespeaks Puerto Rico's American ties. It is identical to a flag devised by local patriots in 1895. The white star symbolizes Puerto Rico, the corners of the blue triangle the legislative, executive and judicial branches of the island's government. Three red stripes symbolize these branches of government and two white stripes stand for the rights of man and freedom of the individual.

Virgin Islands

Pacific Islands

Territory of Guam

Panama Canal Zone

UNITED STATES FLAG CODE

The text of the Flag Code adopted
by Congress in 1942 and amended in 1947

Resolved by the Senate and the House of Representatives of the United States of America that Public Law Numbered 623, approved June 22, 1942, entitled "Joint resolution to codify and emphasize existing rules and customs pertaining to the display and use of the flag of the United States of America," be, and the same is hereby amended to read as follows:

That the following codification of existing rules and customs pertaining to the display and use of the flag of the United States of America be, and it is hereby, established for the use of such civilians or civilian groups or organizations as may not be required to conform with regulations promulgated by one or more executive departments of the Government of the United States.

SEC. 2 (a) It is the universal custom to display the flag only from sunrise to sunset on buildings and on stationary flagstaffs in the open. However, the flag may be displayed at night upon special occasions when it is desired to produce a patriotic effect. (b) The flag should be hoisted briskly and lowered ceremoniously. (c) The flag should not be displayed on days when the weather is inclement.

(d) The flag should be displayed on days when the weather permits, especially on New Year's Day, January 1; Inauguration Day, January 20; Lincoln's Birthday, February 12; Washington's Birthday, February 22; Army Day, April 6; Easter Sunday (variable); Mother's Day, second Sunday in May; Memorial Day (half staff until noon), May 30; Flag

Day, June 14; Independence Day, July 4; Labor Day, first Monday in September; Constitution Day, September 17, Columbus Day, October 12; Navy Day, October 27; Veterans' Day, November 11; Thanksgiving Day, fourth Thursday in November; Christmas Day, December 25; such other days as may be proclaimed by the President of the United States; the birthdays of States (dates of admission); and on the State holidays.

(e) The flag should be displayed daily, weather permitting, on or near the main administration building of every public institution (f) The flag should be displayed in or near every polling place on election days. (g) The flag should be displayed during school days in or near every schoolhouse.

SEC. 3. That the flag, when carried in a procession with another flag or flags, should be either on the marching right; that is, the flag's own right, or, if there is a line of other flags, in front of the center of that line. (a) The flag should not be displayed on a float in a parade except from a staff, or as provided in subsection (i). (b) The flag should not be draped over the hood, top, sides, or back of a vehicle or of a railroad train or a boat. When the flag is displayed on a motorcar, the staff shall be fixed firmly to the chasis or clamped to the radiator cap.

(c) No other flag or pennant should be placed above or, if on the same level, to right of the flag of the United States of America, except during church services conducted by naval chaplains at sea, when the church pennant may be flown above the flag during church services for the personnel of the Navy. No person shall display the flag of the United Nations or any other national or international flag equal, above, or in a position of superior prominence or honor to or in place of, the flag of the United States at any place within the United States or any Territory or possession thereof: *Provided*, That nothing in this section shall make unlawful the continuance of the practice heretofore followed of displaying the flag of the

United Nations in a position of superior prominence or honor, and other national flags in positions of equal prominence or honor, with that of the flag of the United States at the headquarters of the United Nations.

(d) The flag of the United States of America, when it is displayed with another flag against a wall from crossed staffs should be on the right, the flag's own right, and its staff should be in front of the staff of the other flag. (e) The flag of the United States of America should be at the center and at the highest point of the group when a number of flags of States or localities or pennants of societies are grouped and displayed from staffs. (f) When flags of States, cities, or localities, or pennants of societies are flown on the same halyard with the flag of the United States, the latter should always be at the peak. When the flags are flown from adjacent staffs, the flag of the United States should be hoisted first and lowered last. No such flag or pennant may be placed above the flag of the United States or to the right of the flag of the United States. (g) When flags of two or more nations are displayed, they are to be flown from separate staffs of the same height. The flags should be approximately equal size. International usage forbids the display of the flag of one nation above that of another nation in time of peace.

(h) When the flag of the United States is displayed from a staff projecting horizontally or at an angle from the window sill, balcony, or front of a building the union of the flag should be placed at the peak of the staff unless the flag is at half staff. When the flag is suspended over a sidewalk from a rope extending from a house to a pole at the edge of the sidewalk, the flag should be hoisted out union first, from the building. (i) When the flag is displayed otherwise than by being flown from a staff, it should be displayed flat, whether indoors or out, or so suspended that its folds fall as free as though the flag were staffed. (j) When the flag is displayed over the middle of the street, it should be suspended vertically with the union to the north in an east and west street or to the east in a north and south street.

(k) When used on a speaker's platform, the flag, if displayed flat, should be displayed above and behind the speaker. When displayed from a staff in a church or public auditorium, if it is displayed in the chancel of a church, or on the speaker's platform in a public auditorium, the flag should occupy the position of honor and be placed at the clergyman's or speaker's right as he faces the congregation or audience. Any other flag so displayed in the chancel or on the platform should be placed at the clergyman's or speaker's left as he facs the congregation or audience. But when the flag is displayed from a staff in a church or public auditorium elsewhere than in the chancel or on the platform it shall be placed in the position of honor at the right of the congregation or audience as they face the chancel or platform. Any other flag so displayed should be placed on the left of the congregation or audience as they face the chancel or platform.

(l) the flag should form a distinctive feature of the ceremony of unveiling a statue or monument, but it should never be used as the covering for the statue or monument.

(m) The flag, when flown at half staff, should be first hoisted to the peak for an instant and then lowered to the half-staff position. The flag should be again raised to the peak before it is lowered for the day. By 'half staff' is meant lowering the flag to one-half the distance between the top and bottom of the staff. Crepe streamers may be affixed to spear heads or flagstaffs in a parade only by order of the President of the United States. (n) When the flag is used to cover a casket, it should be so placed that the union is at the head and over the left shoulder. The flag should not be lowered into the grave or allowed to touch the ground.

SEC. 4. That no disrespect should be shown to the flag of the United States of America; the flag should not be dipped to any person or thing. Regimental colors, State flags, and or-

126

ganization or institutional flags are to be dipped as a mark of honor. (a) The flag should never be displayed with the union down save as a signal of dire distress. (b) The flag should never touch anything beneath it, such as the ground, the floor, water, or merchandise. (c) The flag should never be carried flat or horizontally, but always aloft and free. (d) The flag should never be used as drapery of any sort whatsoever, never festooned, drawn back, nor up, in folds; but always allowed to fall free. Bunting of blue, white, and red always arranged with the blue above, the white in the middle, and the red below, should be used for covering a speaker's desk, draping the front of a platform, and for decoration in general (e) The flag should never be fastened, displayed, used, or stored in such a manner as will permit it to be easily torn, soiled, or damaged in any way. (f) The flag should never be used as a covering for a ceiling. (g) The flag should never have placed upon it, nor on any part of it, nor attached to it any mark, insignia, letter, word, figure, design, picture, or drawing of any nature. (h) The flag should never be used as a receptacle for receiving, holding, carrying, or delivering anything. (i) The flag should never be used for advertising purposes in any manner whatsoever. It should not be embroidered on such articles as cushions or handkerchiefs and the like, printed or otherwise impressed on paper napkins or boxes or anything that is designed for temporary use and discard; or used as any portion of a costume or athletic uniform. Advertising signs should not be fastened to a staff or halyard from which the flag is flown.

(j) The flag, when it is in such condition that it is no longer a fitting emblem for display, should be destroyed in a dignified way, preferably by burning.

SEC. 5. That during the ceremony of hoisting or lowering the flag or when the flag is passing in a parade or in a review, all persons present should face the flag, stand at attention, and salute. Those present in uniform should render the military salute. When not in uniform, men should remove the head-dress with the right hand holding it at the left shoulder, the hand being over the heart. Men without hats should salute in the same manner. Aliens should stand at attention. Women should salute by placing the right hand over the heart. The salute to the flag in the moving column should be rendered at the moment the flag passes.

SEC. 6. That when the national anthem is played and the flag is not displayed, all present should stand and face toward the music. Those in uniform should salute at the first note of the anthem, retaining this position until the last note. All others should stand at attention, men removing the head-dress. When the flag is displayed, all present should face the flag and salute.

SEC. 7. That the following is designated as the pledge of allegiance to the flag: 'I pledge allegiance to the flag of the United States of America and to the Republic for which it stands, one Nation under God, indivisible, with liberty and justice for all.' Such pledge should be rendered by standing with the right hand over the heart. However, civilians will always show full respect to the flag when the pledge is given by merely standing at attention, men removing the headdress. Persons in uniform shall render the military salute.

SEC. 8. Any rule or custom pertaining to the display of the flag of the United States of America, set forth herein, may be altered, modified, or repealed, or additional rules with respect thereto may be prescribed, by the Commander in Chief of the Army and Navy of the United States, whenever he deems it to be appropriate or desirable; and any such altera-tion or additional rule shall be set forth in a proclamation.